Explore new ideas!

Welcome to

Getting to Know Us

Read exciting literature, science and social studies texts!

Become an expert writer!

Build vocabulary and knowledge to unlock the Wonders of reading!

 Use your student login to explore your interactive Reading/Writing Workshop, practice close reading, and more.

Go Digital! www.connected.mcgraw-hill.com

Cover and Title pages: Nathan Love

www.mheonline.com/readingwonders

Copyright © 2017 McGraw-Hill Education

All rights reserved. No part of this publication may be reproduced or distributed in any form or by any means, or stored in a database or retrieval system, without the prior written consent of McGraw-Hill Education, including, but not limited to, network storage or transmission, or broadcast for distance learning.

Send all inquiries to:
McGraw-Hill Education
2 Penn Plaza
New York, NY 10121

ISBN: 978-0-07-672712-4
MHID: 0-07-672712-2

Printed in the United States of America.

5 6 7 8 9 LKV 29 28 27 26 25

Wonders

An English Language Arts Program

Program Authors

Diane August
Donald R. Bear
Janice A. Dole
Jana Echevarria
Douglas Fisher
David Francis
Vicki Gibson

Jan Hasbrouck
Margaret Kilgo
Jay McTighe
Scott G. Paris
Timothy Shanahan
Josefina V. Tinajero

Unit 1

Getting to Know Us

The Big Idea
What makes you special?.... 6

Week 1 · At School   8

Words to Know 10
Phonics: Short a 12
Jack Can
   Realistic Fiction 14
Comprehension Skill: Key Details 24
Writing and Grammar: Informative Text 26

Week 2 · Where I Live   28

Words to Know 30
Phonics: Short i 32
Six Kids
   Fantasy 34
Comprehension Skill: Key Details 44
Writing and Grammar: Informative Text 46

Go Digital! www.connected.mcgraw-hill.com

Week 3 · Our Pets 48

Words to Know 50
Phonics: l-blends 52
A Pig for Cliff
Fantasy 54
Comprehension Skill: Key Details 64
Writing and Grammar: Narrative Text 66

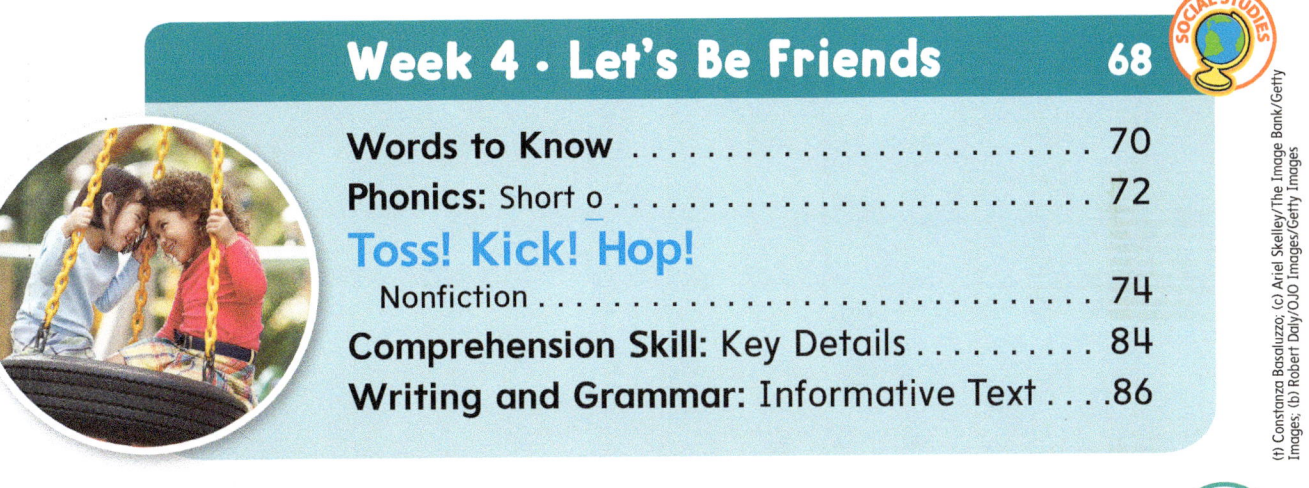

Week 4 · Let's Be Friends 68

Words to Know 70
Phonics: Short o 72
Toss! Kick! Hop!
Nonfiction 74
Comprehension Skill: Key Details 84
Writing and Grammar: Informative Text 86

Week 5 · Let's Move! 88

Words to Know 90
Phonics: r-blends, s-blends 92
Move and Grin!
Nonfiction 94
Comprehension Skill: Key Details 104
Writing and Grammar: Informative Text 106

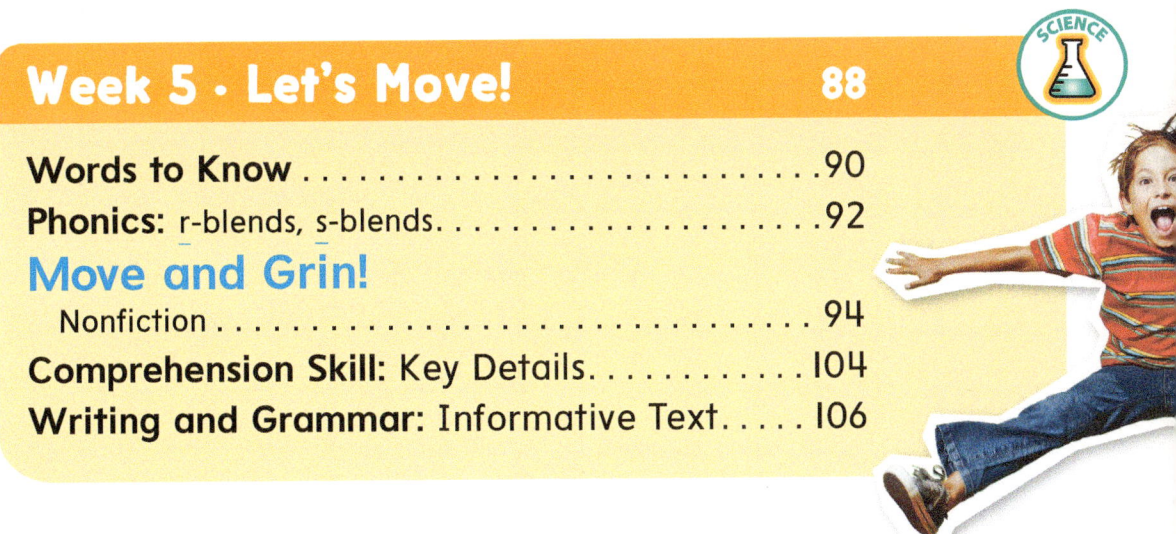

Unit 1

Getting to Know Us

Something About Me

There's something about me

That I'm knowing.

There's something about me

That isn't showing.

I'm growing!

The Big Idea

What makes you special?

Words to Know

does

Dan **does** his best work.

not

Do **not** run at school.

school

We read a lot in **school**.

what

What can we play today?

Your Turn

Say the sentence for each word. Then make up another sentence.

Go Digital! Use the online visual glossary

Phonics/Fluency

Short a

The letter a can make the short a sound in **pack**.

ax	can	sad
fan	hat	jam
pan	ran	map
tack	back	wag

Nan ran back to the mat.

Nan sat on the mat.

Your Turn

Look for these words with short a in "Jack Can."

Jack   can   Max

sad   Nan

Genre Realistic Fiction

Essential Question

What do you do at your school?

Read about what friends can do at school.

Go Digital!

Max can.

Can Jack? Jack can.

Max can. Can Jack?

Jack can **not**.

Jack is sad.

What does Nan do?

Nan helps Jack!

Jack likes school.

Comprehension

Key Details

Key details help you understand a story.

Words and pictures in a story give you the key details.

🔍 Find Text Evidence

Find key details about what Jack can do.

page 17

Can Jack? Jack can.

Detail	Detail	Detail
Jack can make a picture of himself.	Jack can not reach.	Nan helps Jack reach.

Your Turn

Talk about key details in "Jack Can."

Go Digital! Use the interactive graphic organizer

Writing and Grammar

Write About the Text

Pages 14–23

Matt

I answered the question: **Which activity seems most challenging for Jack? How does this change?**

Student Model: *Informative Text*

Jack can not write a word.
Jack can not reach up.
I see that Jack is too short.

Clues
I used evidence from the story's words and pictures.

This makes Jack sad.
Nan gets a stool for Jack.
Now Jack can reach.

Grammar
A **sentence** begins with a capital letter.

Focus on an Event
I wrote about when Jack got help.

Your Turn

How do Jack's feelings about school change? Use text evidence to support your answer.

Go Digital!
Write your response online.
Use your editing checklist.

Weekly Concept Where I Live

Essential Question
What is it like where you live?

Go Digital!

Outside My Window

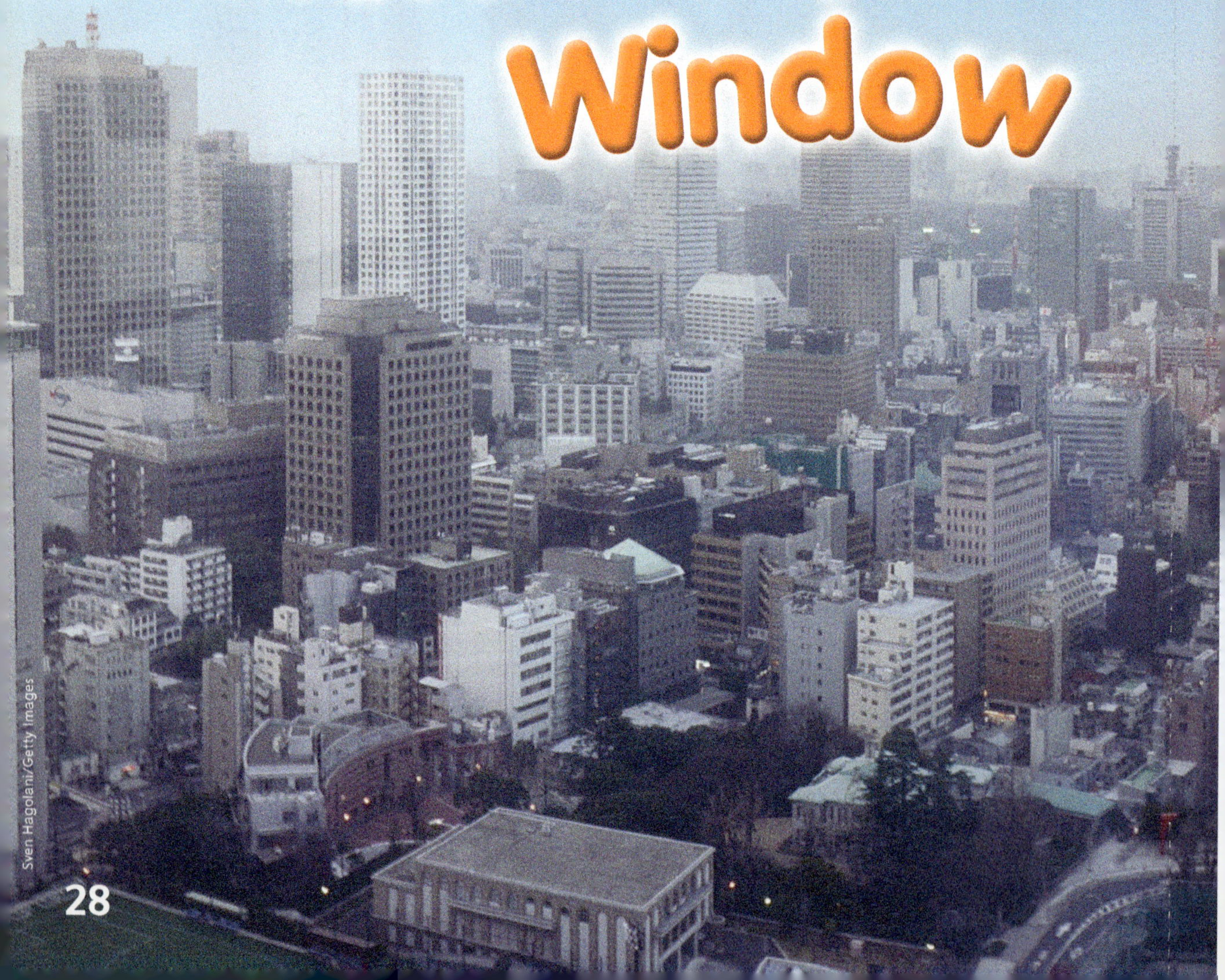

Talk About It

What does the boy see outside his window?

Words to Know

down

We go **down** the steps.

out

They go **out** to play.

up

They went **up** the hill.

very

It is **very** loud in the city.

Your Turn

Say the sentence for each word. Then make up another sentence.

Go Digital! Use the online visual glossary

Short i

The letter i can make the short i sound in **six**.

it	is	sit
him	big	dip
kid	pig	lid
sick	kiss	miss

Nick ran up a big hill.

Will he sit with Jill?

Your Turn

Look for these words with short i in "Six Kids."

six   kids   hill   dig

pick   dip   will   fix   it

Genre Fantasy

Essential Question

What is it like where you live?

Read about what an animal family does where they live.

Go Digital!

Six kids go **out**.

Six kids go **up** a hill.

Six kids dig, dig, dig.

Six kids go **down**.

Six kids pick, pick, pick.

Six kids are **very** blue.

Six kids dip, dip, dip.

That will fix it.

Six kids like it here!

Comprehension

Key Details

Key details help you understand a story.

The sequence is the order in which the key details happen.

🔍 Find Text Evidence

Find a key detail about what the six kids do first.

page 37

Six kids go **up** a hill.

Detail	Detail	Detail
First six chicks walk up a hill carrying farm tools.	Then they dig holes to plant seeds in their garden.	Then the six chicks pick blueberries.

Your Turn

What happens next? Talk about other key details in "Six Kids."

Go Digital! Use the interactive graphic organizer

Writing and Grammar

Write About the Text

Pages 34–43

Sasha

I responded to the prompt: **Describe where the six kids live.**

Student Model: *Narrative Text*

The six kids live on a farm.
The farm is on a big hill.
The grass is green.

Details
I used details to describe the farm.

Grammar
The **words** are in the correct **order**. The sentence makes sense.

There are lots of berries.
The farm is near a pond.

Clues
I figured out more about the farm from the picture on page 40.

Your Turn

Describe how where the six kids live affects what they do. Use text evidence to support your answer.

Go Digital!
Write your response online.
Use your editing checklist.

Special Friends

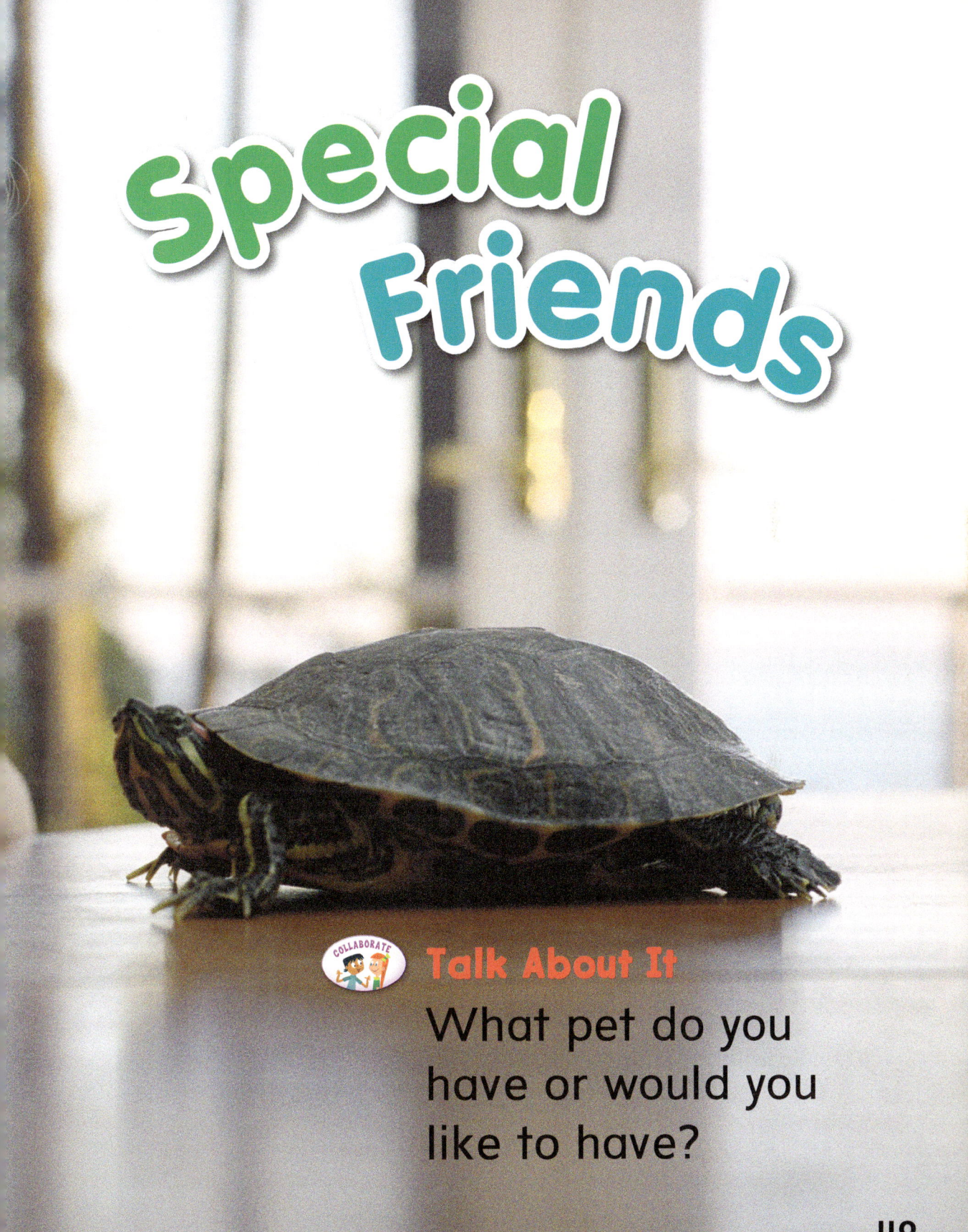

Talk About It

What pet do you have or would you like to have?

Words to Know

be

A turtle can **be** a fun pet.

come

My bunny will **come** to eat.

good

A cat is a **good** pet.

pull

I **pull** my dog in a wagon.

Your Turn

Say the sentence for each word. Then make up another sentence.

Go Digital! Use the online visual glossary

Phonics/Fluency

l-blends

The letters bl, cl, fl, gl, pl, and sl make the beginning sounds in **black**, **click**, **flat**, **glad**, **plan**, and **slim**.

flap	slips	flag
glass	blip	clap
class	flips	blab
plans	slick	slam

Our class pet is named Slick.

Slick can flip in its glass bowl!

Your Turn

Look for these words with l-blends in "A Pig for Cliff."

Cliff	glad	Slim
black	slam	slip

Genre Fantasy

Essential Question

What makes a pet special?
Read about Cliff's new pet.

Go Digital!

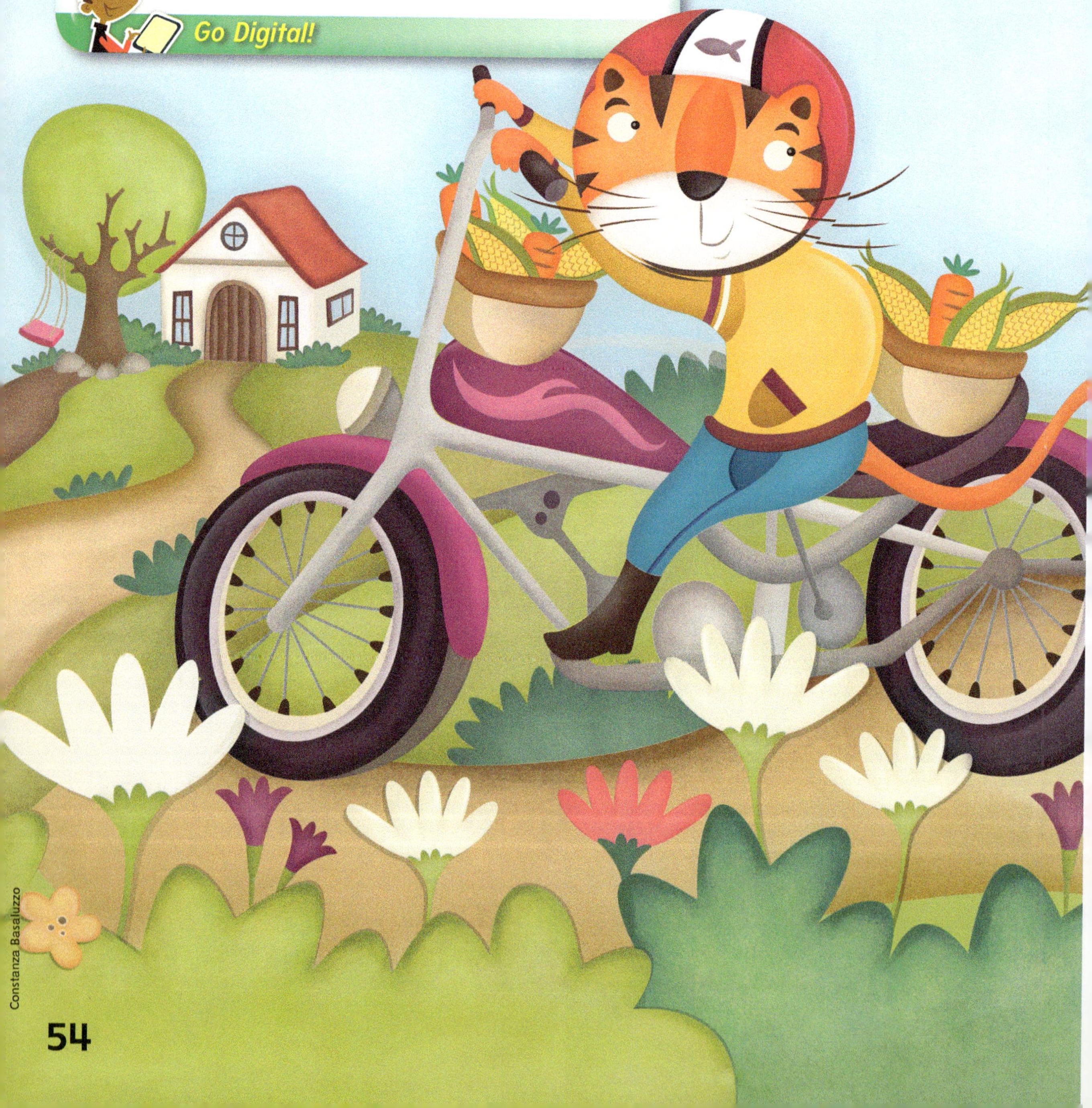

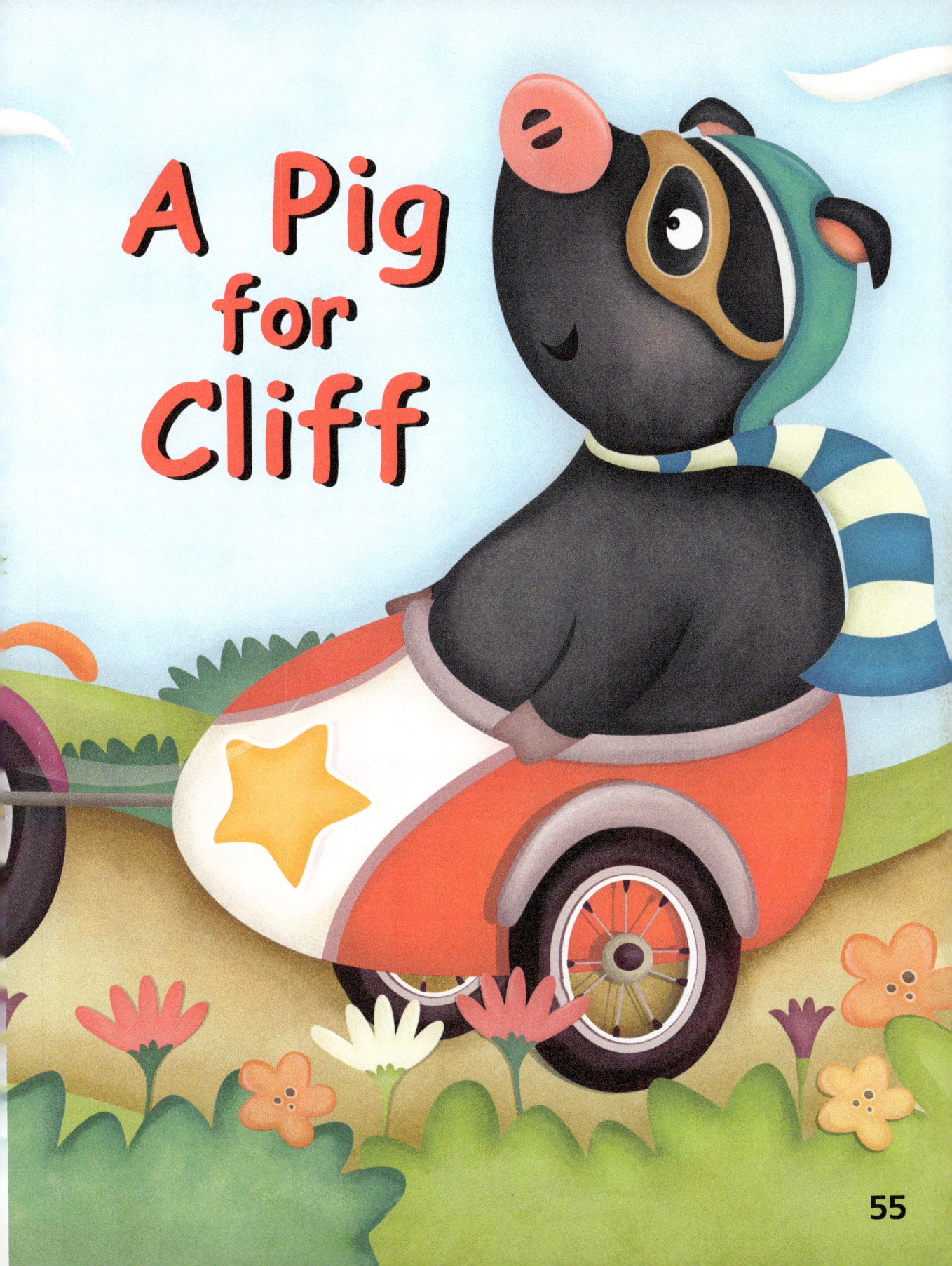

Cliff is glad.

Cliff has a new pet.

It is Slim.

It is a big black pig.

Slim can not fit in!

Come out, Slim!

Slam!

Cliff can not sit with Slim.

Cliff and Slim slip.

Slim can go up.

Cliff can not.

Slim can **pull** Cliff.

Slim will **be** a **good** pet!

Comprehension

Key Details

Key details help you understand a story.

Key details happen in order, or in sequence.

🔍 Find Text Evidence

Find a key detail in the story.

page 57

It is Slim.
It is a big black pig.

Detail	Detail	Detail
Cliff has a big, black pet pig named Slim.	Slim breaks the swing, so Cliff and Slim fall in the mud.	Slim pulls Cliff up out of the mud. Slim is a good pet.

Your Turn

Talk about your favorite details in "A Pig for Cliff." Tell about them in order.

Go Digital! Use the interactive graphic organizer

Writing and Grammar

Write About the Text

Pages 54–63

Marco

I responded to the prompt: **Write a new story in which Cliff brings home a different pet.**

Student Model: *Narrative Text*

Cliff has a new pet dog, Max.
→ Max loves to tap dance!

Cliff does not tap dance.
→ Cliff gets on his bike.

Characters
I created a make-believe character. I told what he likes.

Describing Details
I told what the character does.

Cliff comes back.

He has new tap shoes.

Max and Cliff dance all day!

Grammar

A sentence that tells something and ends with a period is a **statement**.

Your Turn

Write a new story for Cliff and Slim. How do they get into trouble? How do they get out of it?

Go Digital!
Write your response online.
Use your editing checklist.

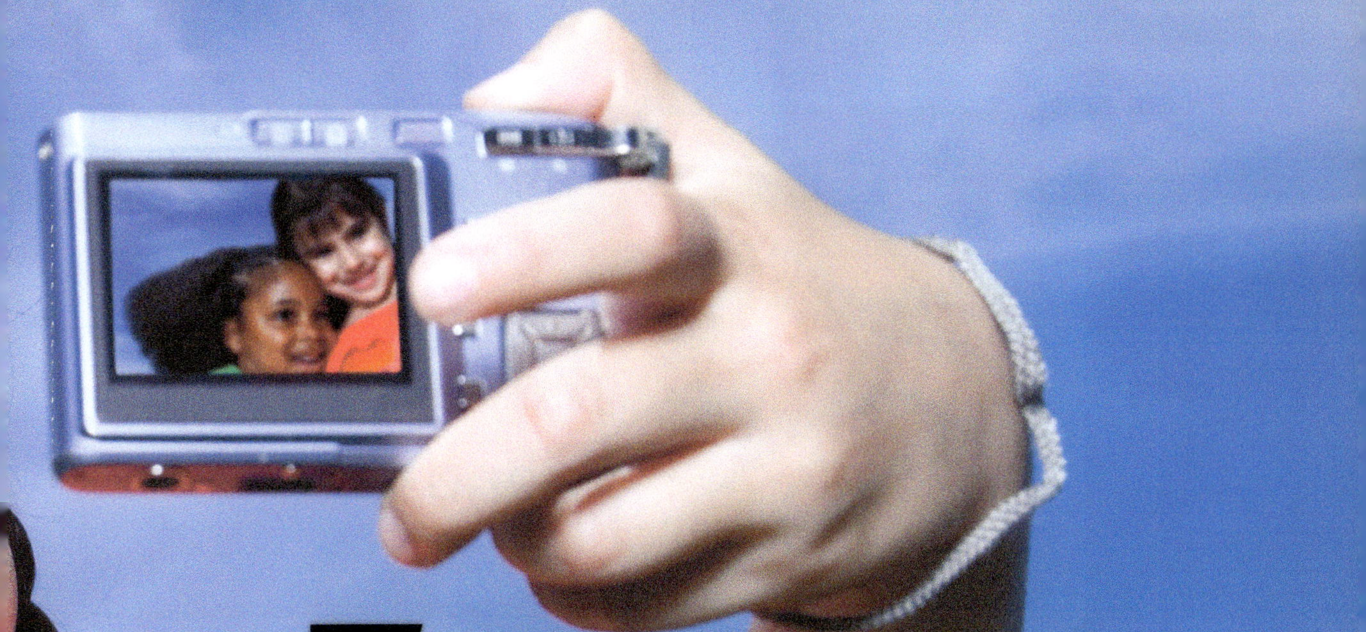

Just for Fun

Talk About It

What do you and your friends do together?

Words to Know

fun

It is **fun** to play tag with friends.

make

We can **make** funny hats.

they

Can **they** go up and down fast?

too

We like to skate, **too**!

Your Turn

Say the sentence for each word. Then make up another sentence.

Go Digital! Use the online visual glossary

Phonics/Fluency

Short o

The letter o can make the short o sound in hop.

box	top	rocks
not	lot	fox
jog	clock	toss
dolls	hot	mops

Can Ron jog on a hot day?

Ron can jog a lot!

Your Turn

Look for these words with short o in "Toss! Kick! Hop!"

toss   hop   block

dolls   flop

Genre Nonfiction

Essential Question

What do friends do together?

Read about how friends play together.

Go Digital!

Toss! Kick! Hop!

Kids play together.

Kids zip, zip, zip.

Kids toss, toss, toss.

Kids kick, kick, kick, **too**!

Kids **make** block houses.

Kids make dolls.

Kids hop in sacks.

Hop, hop, flop!

They have **fun!**

Comprehension

Key Details

Key **details** tell important information about the selection.

You can use photos to learn key details.

🔍 **Find Text Evidence**

Find a key detail that tells about one way that friends play together. Use the words and pictures.

page 78

Kids toss, toss, toss.

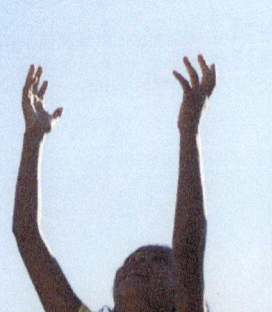

Detail	Detail	Detail
Kids toss balls.	Kids make dolls.	Kids hop in sacks.

Your Turn

Talk about other key details in "Toss! Kick! Hop!"

Go Digital! Use the interactive graphic organizer

Writing and Grammar

Write About the Text

Pages 74–83

Penny

I responded to the prompt: **Write a new title for the selection. Tell how it is different from the original.**

Student Model: *Informative Text*

My title is "Fun With Friends."
The old title is about moves.
The kids do more than move.
The kids play together.

Compare and Contrast
I told how I made my title different.

Read Together

Clues
I used evidence from the text and photos to tell that the kids make things.

They make houses and dolls.
The kids smile and laugh too.
They have fun with friends!

Grammar
An **exclamation** shows strong feelings and ends with an exclamation mark.

Your Turn

Look at the different things that the children are doing to have fun. How are they the same? How are they different? Use text evidence to support your answer.

Go Digital!
Write your response online.
Use your editing checklist.

Weekly Concept Let's Move!

Essential Question
How does your body move?

Go Digital!

Ready, Set, Move!

Talk About It

How are these kids using their bodies?

Words to Know

jump

Do you like to **jump**?

move

It is fun to **move** to music.

run

My dog can **run** fast.

two

The **two** cats like to play.

Your Turn

Say the sentence for each word. Then make up another sentence.

Go Digital! Use the online visual glossary

Phonics/Fluency

r-blends, s-blends

The letters br, cr, dr, fr, gr, pr, tr, sk, sm, sn, sp, st, and sw make the beginning sounds in **brick, crab, drip, frog, grass, prop, trap, skin, smack, sniff, spot, still,** and **swam.**

brag	crib	drop
grab	swims	track
skips	snaps	stop
trip	stick	spill

Fran can run, spin, and skip.

Gram stops to see Fran's trick.

Your Turn

Look for these words with r-blends and s-blends in "Move and Grin!"

grin	frog	Scott	
swim	Fran	trot	
Stan	crab	grab	Skip

Genre Nonfiction

Essential Question

How does your body move?
Read about how animals and kids move.

Go Digital!

Scott's frog can hop and **jump**.

It can **move** its back legs.

Scott can hop and jump, too.

Hop, hop, jump.

Fran's dog can swim a lot.

It kicks its **two** front legs.

Fran can swim a lot, too.

Swim, swim, swim.

Stan's horse can trot and **run**.

It jogs on its big long legs.

Stan can trot and run, too.

Trot, trot, run.

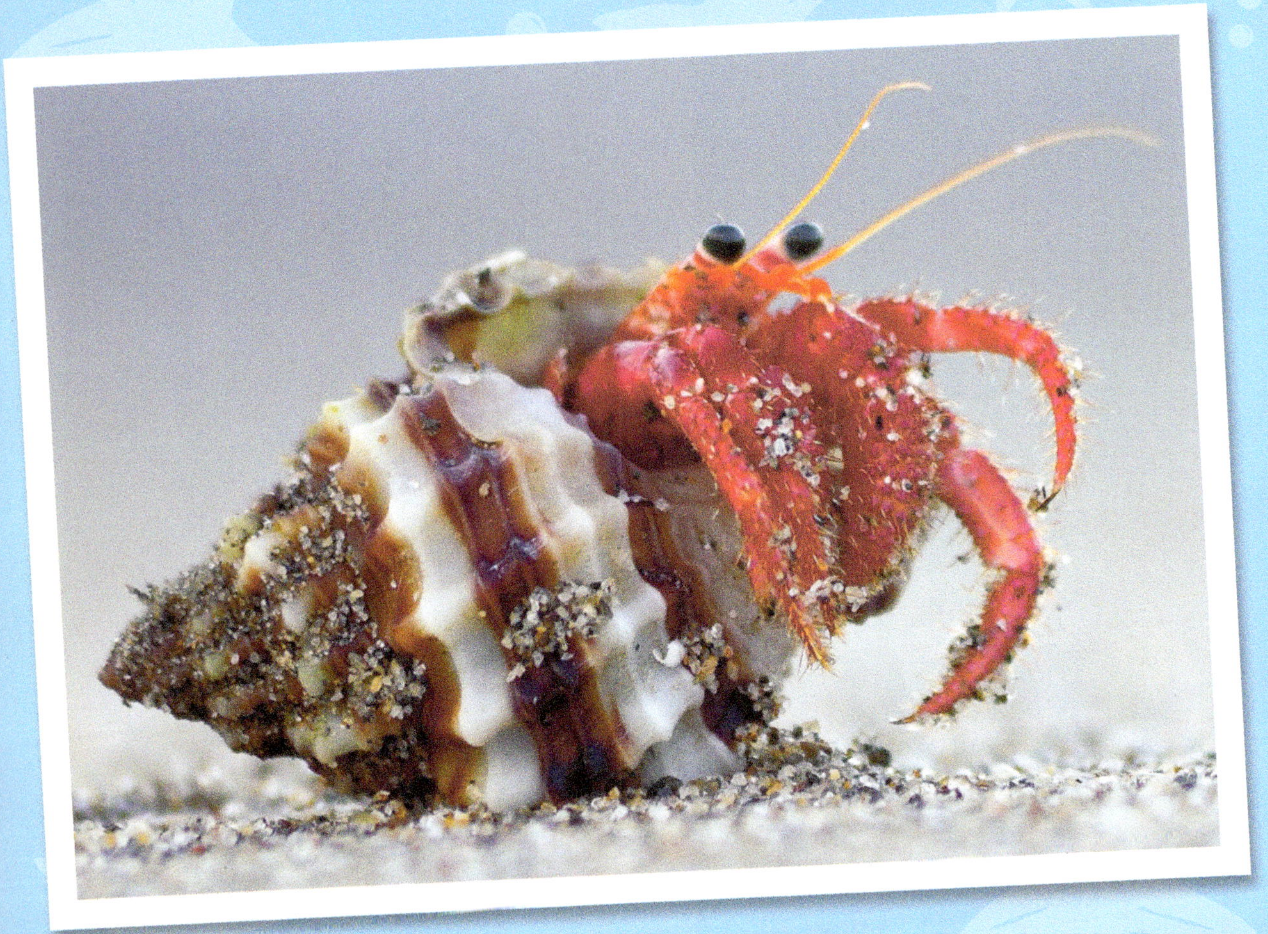

Antonio Luis Martinez Cano/Moment/Getty Images

Skip's crab can grab.

It can grab with its claw.

Grab, grab, grab.

Skip can grab, too.

Grab, grab, grab.

What can Skip grab with?

Comprehension

Key Details

Key details tell important information about the selection.

You can use words and photos to learn key details.

 Find Text Evidence

Find key details that tell how Fran's dog moves. Use the words and pictures.

page 98

Fran's dog can swim a lot.

It kicks its **two** front legs.

Detail	Detail
Fran's dog can swim.	It kicks its two front legs.

Your Turn

Talk about the key details in "Move and Grin!"

Go Digital! Use the interactive graphic organizer

Writing and Grammar

Write About the Text

Pages 94–103

Rose

I answered the question: **What steps does Skip take to reach up high? Use first, next, then, and last.**

Student Model: *Informative Text*

This is how Skip reaches.
First, Skip looks up.
Next, Skip lifts his arm.

Clues
I used the photo to answer the question.

Order of Events
I told things that Skip does in the **order** he does them.

Read Together

Then, Skip raises his foot.
Last, he grabs with his hand.

Grammar

This sentence is a **statement** telling what Skip does.

Your Turn

Use <u>first</u>, <u>next</u>, <u>then</u>, and <u>last</u> to describe the steps needed to make Fran's motions. Use text evidence to support your answer.

Go Digital!
Write your response online.
Use your editing checklist.